SICILY TRAVEL GUIDE 2024

Sicily Odyssey:

Crafting Your Epic Journey in the Year 2024

STELLA ARCHER

All Rights Reserved. No part of this book may be reproduced, stored in a retrieval system, or transmitted in any form or by any means, electronic, mechanical, photocopying, recording, or otherwise, without written permission from the publisher. Copyright ©[2023][Stella Archer] All Rights Reserved.

TABLE OF CONTENTS

OVERVIEW

CHAPTER 1
Sicily Unveiled

CHAPTER 2
PRACTICAL ADVICE: Important Travel Information and Recommendations

CHAPTER 3
SIGHTSEEING AND ATTRACTIONS: Discovering Sicily's Hidden Treasures with Recommendations

CHAPTER 4
ACCOMMODATIONS IN SICILY: Relaxing Retreats with Recommendations

CHAPTER 5
MEDIEVAL MARVELS: Towns Frozen in Time

CHAPTER 6
DINING AND ENTERTAINMENT: Savoring Sicilian Delights

CHAPTER 7
TRANSPORT: Understanding Sicily's Networks

CHAPTER 8
RETAIL THERAPY: Sicilian Style Shopping

CHAPTER 9
ITINERARIES AND TOURS: Crafting Your Sicilian Experience

CHAPTER 10
LOCAL TIPS AND INSIGHTS: Unearthing Sicily's Secrets

CHAPTER 11
USEFUL PHRASES: Speaking Sicilian

CHAPTER 12
YOUR SICILIAN ODYSSEY MEMORIES: Reflection and Farewell

OVERVIEW

A place rich in history, culture, and natural beauty can be found in the center of the Mediterranean, and it has long captured the attention of tourists. Please enjoy your stay at "Sicily Odyssey: Crafting Your Epic Journey in the Year 2024."

In this thorough travel guide, I cordially invite you to set out on a memorable journey through the alluring island of Sicily, where ancient ruins bear witness to millennia of civilization, where vivacious traditions coexist with contemporary sensibilities, and where a variety of landscapes, from rocky mountains to azure coastlines, provide an unrivaled setting for your exploration.

Unquestionably captivating, Sicily is a tapestry made of the threads of history, art, food, and natural beauty. You'll discover the soul of Sicily as you browse through the pages of this manual thanks to thoughtfully chosen insights and helpful suggestions.

No matter if you are an experienced traveler or setting off on your first international trip, the "Sicily Odyssey" is your compass, guiding you on a life-changing adventure that goes beyond ordinary travel.

My voyage around Sicily is organized to provide you with a smooth journey, a guide to both the well-traveled path and the undiscovered treasure that characterizes this complex island.

I explore several facets of the Sicilian experience in each chapter, giving you a complete toolset to direct your research.

"Sicily Odyssey" takes you past the surface and into the core of what makes Sicily remarkable, from the historical marvel of an old temple and medieval city to the sensory thrill of a local market and mouthwatering food.

"Sicily Odyssey" is more than simply a map; it's a travel companion that gives you the freedom to choose your special itinerary.

I urge you to go further even though I give crucial information like travel advice, lodging recommendations, and pragmatic considerations.

Talk to enthusiastic craftspeople, immerse yourself in the culture, and look for a little nook away from the crowds. With plenty of freedom for spontaneity and introspection, you may use this manual as the starting point for your amazing voyage.

Sicily is a constantly changing canvas, painted with the colors of modernity while retaining its historic character, as the year 2024 progresses.

The knowledge and insight provided in "Sicily Odyssey" are grounded in the present and provide you with a current-day view of the island.

I recognize the ephemeral nature of travel, too, and I urge you to double-check the information as you plan your trip because advice and situations are prone to change.

As varied and rich as the island itself is the voyage that lies ahead. "Sicily Odyssey" is your compass, your guide, and your source of inspiration, whether you're an art enthusiast drawn to Caravaggio's work and ancient mosaics, a history nerd eager to explore the ruins of an ancient civilization, a foodie ready to indulge in Sicilian culinary delight, or simply a traveler seeking authentic connection.

So, turning the page and starting your Sicilian trip with an open mind and a curious spirit is my invitation to you.

This journey has the promise of discovery, enlightenment, and lifelong memories. As you set out on "Sicily Odyssey: Crafting Your Epic Journey in the Year 2024," embrace the past, enjoy the present, and forge ahead.

SICILY MAP

SICILY FLAG

CHAPTER 1

Sicily Unveiled

Sicily is a magical island treasure in the center of the Mediterranean, nestled at the confluence of history, culture, and breathtaking natural scenery.

Here, the ancient and the modern coexist, bustling towns coexist with ancient ruins, and visitors from all over the world are warmly welcomed by the local culture.

Layers of Civilization: A View into Sicilian History

Sicily's history is a complex tapestry made from the threads of several civilizations that have permanently etched their imprints on its surface.

Each historical period has contributed to the island's distinctive personality, from the ancient Greeks to the Romans, from the Byzantines to the Normans.

Ancient temples, well-preserved theaters, and medieval fortifications that stand as witnesses to the passage of time are among the landscape's dispersed reminders of their existence.

The Sicilian Experience: A Cultural Melting Pot

The rich cultural legacy of the island is a harmonious fusion of many influences. Due to its strategic location, Sicily has been sought after by several empires, and with each conquest, a new cultural identity was established.

The architecture, as well as the cuisine, language, and customs, are examples of this mix.

The island hums with a singular cultural life, from the beautiful mosaics of the Norman churches to the fascinating rhythms of traditional Sicilian music.

Geographical Wonders: Enticing Landscapes

Sicily's landscape is breathtakingly diverse. Its interior is dotted with majestic mountains that provide hiking routes that lead to breathtaking views.

Long expanses of sandy beaches and craggy rocks around the coast provide a stunning backdrop to the turquoise Mediterranean seas. The fertile soil in the lush valleys is home to some of Italy's best vineyards and orchards.

Must-See Attractions: Sicilian Icons

Sicily has a wide variety of attractions to suit all tastes. Old Greek remains from the Valley of the *Temples in Agrigento* are on display there, while *Syracuse's old city* preserves a vivid portrait of life there.

Food lovers are drawn to Palermo's busy markets by their colorful displays of regional specialties.

The *Aeolian Islands* include volcanic sceneries and crystalline seas that charm the spirit of people searching for natural beauty.

TEMPLES IN AGRIGENTO

SYRACUSE'S OLD CITY

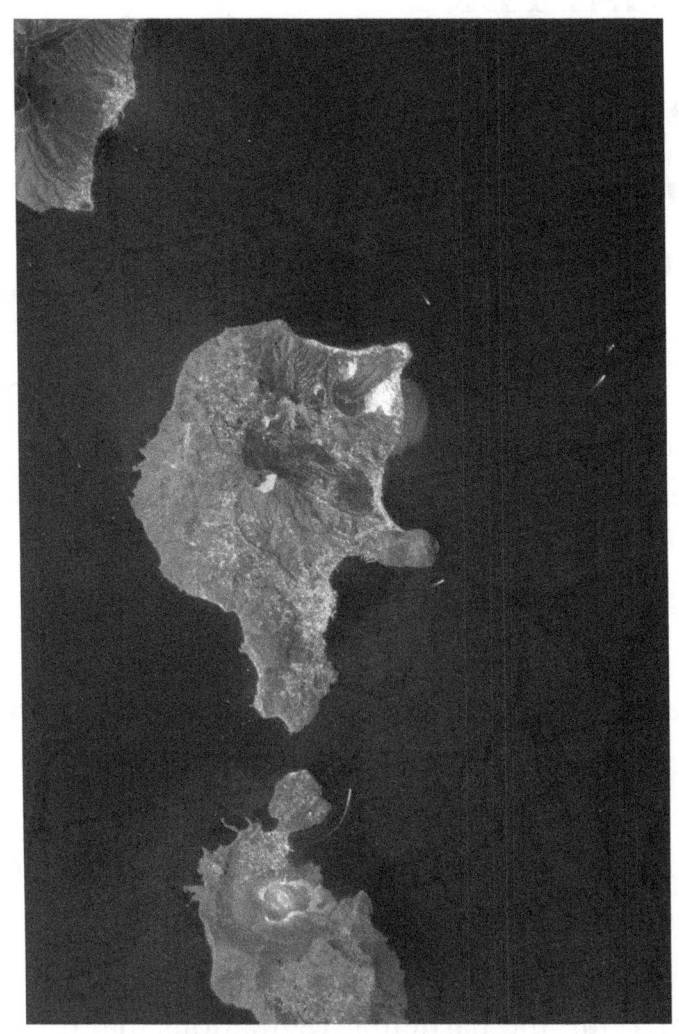

AEOLIAN ISLANDS

CHAPTER 2

PRACTICAL ADVICE: Important Travel Information and Recommendations

Traveling to Sicily is a thrilling experience, and being well-prepared is essential for a seamless trip.

The threshold must be crossed to enter.

Make sure you meet the entrance criteria before setting foot on Sicilian territory.

Italy, of which Sicily is a part, does not require a visa for short-term visitors.

Verifying the particular regulations that relate to your nationality and the length of your intended stay, however, is crucial.

Keep your passport, ID, and any other necessary travel documents close to hand for immigration procedures when you arrive.

Have printed documents of your vacation plans, hotel bookings, and return flight information on hand to speed up the immigration procedure.

This paperwork may be helpful if authorities ask for more details.

Paths to Exploration: Navigating Transportation

The well-connected transportation system in Sicily provides a variety of ways to go about the island.

Major cities are connected by an effective railroad system, making it simple to travel between locations. Access to less-visited locations is made possible by *buses*, providing a window into local life.

BUSES

Renting a car gives you the freedom to explore far-flung areas at your leisure if you're looking for additional flexibility. Ferries link Sicily with other islands, providing options for additional exploration.

22

FERRIES

Consider buying a regional pass for transportation, like a Sicily Rail Pass, which can provide affordable and practical access to numerous modes of transit around the island.

Understanding Local Customs: Cultural Perspectives

Understanding regional customs is crucial for experiencing Sicily to its fullest. Residents of the island take pride in their culture, and it is appreciated when others show them the same courtesy and respect.

Greetings, gestures, and traditions may be different from what you're used to, so taking the time to get to know some fundamental traditions will help you engage with others positively and forge relationships.

Follow local etiquette when eating out by taking your time and having a leisurely dinner.

In Sicilian culture, it is uncommon to rush through a dinner; instead, take your time to taste each course and interact with others.

Language Fundamentals: Interacting in Sicily

English is extensively used in tourist regions even though Italian is the official language. However, knowing a few fundamental Italian words may improve your communication and demonstrate respect for the community.

Simple queries, polite expressions, and terms for dining and shopping may substantially improve your experience and make conversation easier.

To improve communication, we advise you to download a language translation app for your smartphone.

You may get translations even when there is no internet connection thanks to the many applications that provide offline functionality.

Emergency Numbers: Providing Safety

Put your safety first by knowing who to contact in case of emergency. Note down or preserve the local emergency numbers, such as the ones for the police, ambulance, and fire departments.

Additionally, become familiar with the closest embassy or consulate of your own country so that you may contact them in case of emergencies.

For quick access, save emergency contact information in your phone's contacts list.

A tangible copy of these numbers should be included in your travel papers as well.

CHAPTER 3

SIGHTSEEING AND ATTRACTIONS: Discovering Sicily's Hidden Treasures with Recommendations

Welcome to a world filled with amazing marvels and legendary riches.

Sicily's geography is embellished with a tapestry of attractions that are just waiting to be found, including historical monuments, natural wonders, museums, and cultural wonders.

The video game Ancient Marvels: Echoes of Empires

Explore the ancient wonders that have endured the ages as you go back in time. A beautiful collection of **_Doric temples_** from the 5th century BC may be seen at Agrigento's Valley of the Temples, a UNESCO World Heritage Site.

These magnificent remains are evidence of the magnificence of classical Greek architecture and its impact on Sicilian culture.

It is advised to visit the Valley of the Temples during sunrise or sunset to see the structures' mesmerizing shadows against the ***backdrop of the Sicilian sky.***

Cities' Time-Traveling Historical Enclaves

The towns of Sicily are like walking museums, each telling a different story. The **Palazzo dei Normanni**, a historic royal house decorated with the beautiful mosaics of the Cappella Palatina, is located in Palermo, the country's capital.

The historic Greek Theater in Syracuse transports guests back in time to a time when plays reverberated throughout its stone levels.

Discover the *Teatro Antico* in Taormina for breathtaking views of Mount Etna and the Mediterranean and a dramatic performance that combines cultural and environmental elements.

Consider hiring a local guide to reveal the untold tales and historical importance of each historical monument you visit for a more educational experience.

Natural Wonders: Inspiring Landscapes

The Sicilian landscape is a work of art that Mother Nature has painted.

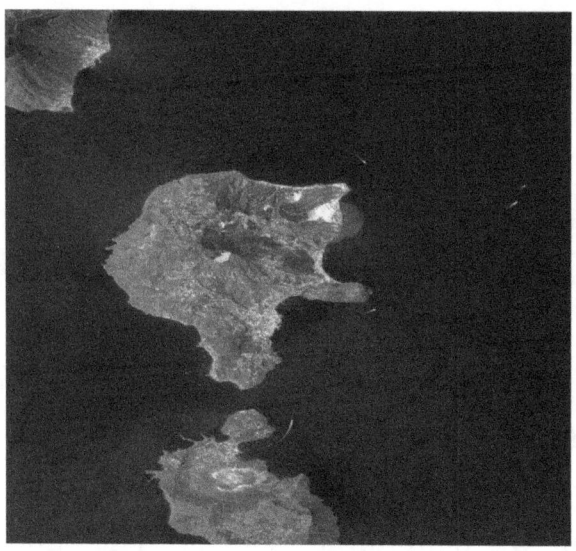

Active volcanoes coexist with blue waters in the volcanic archipelago known as the

Aeolian Islands, a UNESCO Global Geopark.

The eastern horizon is dominated by **Mount Etna**, the tallest active volcano in Europe, which provides chances for trekking that result in panoramic views. The untamed coastline, secret coves, and bright vegetation of the Zingaro Nature Reserve are captivating.

With a skilled guide who can provide insights into Mount Etna's geological beauties, your trek will be both an educational experience and an exhilarating adventure.

Museums and masterpieces: art and culture

Sicily has a rich artistic history that is just waiting to be discovered.

In contrast to the Archaeological *Museum of Syracuse*, which displays ancient artifacts and sculptures, the Museo Regionale di Palermo exhibits works from many historical periods, including classical and modern pieces. The *Monastero dei Benedettini* in Catania is a stunning example of Sicilian Baroque architecture.

MONASTERO DEI BENEDETTINI

Take advantage of the guided tours that several museums provide. Nuanced viewpoints on the artwork, history, and cultural context of each show can be provided by knowledgeable guides.

Spiritual Sanctuaries: Sites for Worship

The religious sites of Sicily provide opportunities for contemplation and awe.

The golden mosaics at the Monreale Cathedral, which represent biblical themes in exquisite detail, amaze.

The architectural fusion on display at the Cattedrale di Palermo reflects the island's long history of absorbing many influences.

GOLDEN MOSAICS

MONREALE CATHEDRAL

For a thorough understanding of the significance of these cathedrals' architecture, art, and religious history, it is advised that you take a guided tour or listen to an audio tour.

Oases of Tranquility: Enchanted Gardens

In Sicily's gorgeous gardens, find solace. In the tranquil setting of *Piazza Armerina*, the Villa Romana del Casale is home to beautifully restored Roman mosaics.

An extensive collection of plants from all over the world may be found in the ***Orto Botanico di Palermo***, a botanical garden established in 1789.

Bring a picnic to enjoy amidst the splendor of these gardens, or take a tour with a guide to learn more about the botanical and historical features of these areas.

Underwater Realms: Marine Splendors

Underwater delights may be found in Sicily for those who are drawn to the ocean.

Ustica's Marine Protected Area features a diverse marine habitat, while Lampedusa's Isola dei Conigli offers the chance to swim with beautiful sea turtles.

To explore the underwater habitats while following ethical environmental standards, reserve a snorkeling or diving tour with trusted local guides.

CHAPTER 4

ACCOMMODATIONS IN SICILY: Relaxing Retreats with Recommendations

Your Sicilian adventure, where the comfort of your stay balances the depth of your investigation, depends on finding the ideal lodging.

Budget-Friendly Gems: Reasonably Priced Comfort

Sicily provides a variety of snug lodging options for guests on a tight budget without sacrificing comfort.

Cities and towns are dotted with hostels and guesthouses that provide gathering places for tourists from all over the world. These inexpensive lodgings offer a venue for intercultural dialogue and shared experiences and frequently come with necessary conveniences like Wi-Fi and community kitchens.

For a genuine taste of Sicily, consider booking a room at a bed and breakfast managed by locals.

Not only will you receive individualized service, but your hosts can also give you priceless insider knowledge about the top restaurants and sights in the area.

Hostel Taormina (Taormina) - This welcoming hostel has a friendly atmosphere and offers both private rooms and inexpensive dorms. situated close to Taormina's center.

HOSTEL TAORMINA

Reviews: Guests like the pleasant personnel, clean amenities, and the opportunity to meet other travelers.

Amenities: Free Wi-Fi, a common living space, and a shared kitchen.

B&B Triskele (Palermo) - This quaint bed and breakfast is well-known for its cozy accommodations and welcoming atmosphere.

B&B TRISKELE (PALERMO)

Reviews: Visitors gush over the hotel's convenient location, kind staff, and the sumptuous breakfast that is given every day.

Amenities: Free city maps, air conditioning, and a complimentary breakfast.

Charming Mid-Range Accommodations: Cozy and Individualistic

Sicily's mid-range lodging combines comfort and personality.

Historic neighborhoods with boutique hotels provide a look into the island's architectural history.

A lot of midrange accommodations include breakfast, WiFi, and maybe even guided excursions or bike rentals to explore the area.

A centrally located hotel will make it simple for you to walk to neighboring landmarks, eateries, and retail establishments.

Hotel Villa Schuler (Taormina)

A charming mid-range hotel located on lush grounds that offers breathtaking views of the Mediterranean Sea.

HOTEL VILLA SCHULER

Reviews: Guests laud the lovely terrace, caring staff, and close access to Taormina's attractions.

Amenities: Beach shuttle service, rooftop garden, on-site restaurant.

Grand Hotel Piazza Borsa (Palermo)

GRAND HOTEL PIAZZA BORSA

In the heart of Palermo, a restored 16th-century edifice houses a historic hotel.

Reviews: Visitors laud the hotel's opulent interior design, spa amenities, and center courtyard with its verdant garden.

Amenities: Fitness facility, rooftop terrace, spa and wellness center.

Opulence and splendor are featured in "Luxury Escapes"

Sicily's luxurious lodgings are lavish havens of comfort and extravagance for visitors looking to indulge.

Five-star resorts and hotels provide panoramic views of the island's breathtaking surroundings or look out over turquoise oceans.

These lodgings offer opulent extras like spa services, fine dining restaurants, and butler services that may accommodate any need.

Ask about special offers or experiences, such as private tours, invitation-only dinners, or spa services using local products, when reserving a luxurious accommodation. These can enrich your Sicilian vacation.

Belmond Villa Sant'Andrea (Taormina)

This luxurious 5-star resort offers a private beach, tasteful accommodations, and panoramic views of the Bay of Mazzar.

Reviews: Visitors laud the excellent cuisine, impeccable service, and breathtaking surroundings. A private beach, infinity pool, and upscale restaurant are available as amenities.

Verdura Resort (Agrigento)

A top-notch luxury resort with a seaside location that offers golf, spa services, and a variety of eating alternatives.

Reviews: Guests are amazed by the expansive grounds, high-quality amenities, and responsive personnel.

Amenities: Private beach, spa, and golf courses of the highest kind.

Agriculture Tourism: Adopting Rural Traditions

Consider vacationing at an agriturismo for a fully immersed experience. These rustic lodgings, which are frequently found on working farms or vineyards, provide a look into Sicilian agricultural life.

Take advantage of meals made with fresh, regional ingredients and engage in farm activities like olive harvesting or wine tasting to get a closer understanding of the island's customs.

To guarantee a room in one of these distinctive and popular hotels, reserve your agriturismo much in advance, particularly during the busiest vacation times.

Agriturismo Gigliotto (Piazza Armerina)

This quaint inn is renowned for its genuine Sicilian food and is bordered by olive orchards and vineyards.

Reviews: Visitors enjoy the tranquil atmosphere, delectable meals, and the chance to experience rural life.

Amenities: On-site dining establishment, wine tasting, cooking demonstrations.

Agriturismo Tenuta Cammarana (Caltagirone)

This charming inn is tucked away in the countryside and offers panoramic views in a tranquil setting.
Reviews: Visitors laud the kind welcome, the roomy accommodations, and the opportunity to relax amid nature.

Amenities: Outdoor terrace, organic farm products, swimming pool.

Apartments and Seaside Villas: A Home Away from Home

The seaside villas and apartments in Sicily are charming and perfect for families and parties.

These lodgings frequently have kitchenettes, allowing you to make meals with the finest regional foods.

Enjoy breathtaking sea views as you awaken and relax in your haven.

CHAPTER 5

MEDIEVAL MARVELS: Towns Frozen in Time

Enter a world where weathered walls bore witness to decades' worth of tales, cobblestone streets whisper secrets of the past, and medieval sounds echo around every corner.

Sicily's medieval cities and villages act as time portals, allowing visitors to immerse themselves in a world of fascinating architecture, deep history, and alluring charm.

Unveiling the past in "A Tapestry of Time"

The historical eras that have shaped Sicily's cultural environment are still evident in the island's medieval towns.

Every cobblestone, archway, and alleyway has a story to tell about the traders, artisans, and conquerors who previously traveled these same roads.

These towns are a tapestry made from the threads of several civilizations, from the Arabian influences of Palermo to the Norman beauty of Cefalù.

Stunning Architecture: "Walking through Time"

Sicily's medieval towns' magnificent structures are examples of the beauty and skill of earlier times.

The **Baroque architecture** in Ragusa Ibla radiates beauty, while the stone buildings in Erice take tourists to a time of forts and castles. Taormina's ancient Greek theater is a testament to the island's everlasting love for artistic expression.

Markets and Plazas: The Centers of Life

Bustling markets and attractive plazas served as the throbbing core of daily life in the center of these medieval cities.

Siracusa's Piazza Duomo emits bustling energy from its local markets, and Modica's squares beckon you to sample regional specialties.

You can see the merging of the present and the past as you stroll around these plazas, where contemporary eateries coexist with iconic sites from the past.

Erice

From its hilltop perch, Erice provides breathtaking panoramic vistas and a maze of medieval alleyways. Visit the Venus Castle and stroll around the quaint shops that line the streets.

Cefalù

Take in the stunning architecture of the city's cathedral and take a stroll through the old streets that lead to the water.

Ragusa Ibla

Get lost in the city's winding lanes lined with Baroque buildings and inviting cafes. Don't overlook San Giorgio's magnificent Cathedral.

Taormina

Admire the beauty of the ancient Greek theater there before taking a stroll through the charming streets and down the renowned Corso Umberto.

Culinary Traditions: Local Flavors

The architecturally stunning medieval cities of Sicily also provide an opportunity to sample the island's delectable cuisine.

Each town has a rich culinary history that has been passed down through the generations, from the world-famous chocolate of Modica to the delicious seafood of Ortigia.

CHAPTER 6

DINING AND ENTERTAINMENT: Savoring Sicilian Delights

As you travel into the heart of Sicily on a culinary and cultural tour, get ready to satisfy your senses.

The Art of Dining: An Experience in Culture

In Sicily, eating is more than just a way to sate your stomach—it's a social activity that immerses you in the local culture.

Take your time when eating at neighborhood restaurants; food is meant to be enjoyed and shared. The congenial setting and engaging discussion add to the allure of Sicilian dining.

Dining Etiquette: Embrace Local Customs

Understanding a few eating customs will help you fully immerse yourself in the Sicilian dining experience.

Take advantage of aperitivi, which are typically little nibbles that go with drinks, while you wait for your meal.

It's typical to eat slowly and with a variety of dishes, from antipasti to dolci (desserts).

Although it is always appreciated, keep in mind that service charges frequently include a gratuity.

Understanding and following local dining etiquette when dining in Sicily improves your experience and enables you to fully immerse yourself in the island's culture.

Here are some important dining etiquette guidelines to remember:

Arrival and Greeting: - Sicilians frequently savor their meals slowly and with company. Although it is appreciated if you arrive on time, don't be shocked if the lunch begins a little later than expected.

As you enter the restaurant or your hosts' home, ***say "buonasera" (Italian for "good evening") or "buongiorno" (Good Day) to them.***

Table Etiquette: You should pace yourself because typical Sicilian feasts include many courses.

It's acceptable to pause between meals to appreciate the flavors and converse with others.

Before you start eating, wait for the host or hostess to extend the invitation.

Sharing and Communal Eating: Sicilians frequently share meals when dining, which promotes a sense of community.

Allow your neighbors to serve themselves by passing them plates before you take your own.
Accepting a taste of someone else's food is a gesture of friendship and hospitality.

Bread with extra virgin olive oil: Sicilians frequently have bread on their tables. It is usual to break off tiny pieces when food is presented and use them to scoop up sauces or olive oil.

Use caution when dipping your bread in the olive oil and use a separate plate instead of the shared one.

Express Appreciation: Compliment the chef or host on the meal.

A way to show gratitude for the work that was put into cooking the meal is to express how much you enjoyed the food.

Gratuities: Gratuities are customarily left at restaurants and range from 10% to 15% of the total bill.

Before leaving a bigger tip, double-check to see whether there is a service charge at the establishment.

Drinking wine and toasting: It is usual to raise your glass and make eye contact with everyone at the table when making a toast.

A toast should always be accepted with a glass raised and a "salute" (to your health).

Pleasingness and Gratitude: Thankfulness and politeness go a long way.

If you want something or want someone to know you appreciate something, use "per favor" (please) and "grazie" (thank you).

Engage in discussion with locals and other diners; you might end up learning more about the island's culture and forming new acquaintances as a result.

Culinary Treasures: Delightful Dishes

The numerous influences and lengthy history of Sicily are reflected in its cuisine.

Every bite has a unique flavor, from the bold flavors of street cuisine to the sophistication of classic recipes.

Enjoy pasta alla Norma, a dish named after an opera and containing eggplant, tomato sauce, and ricotta salata, or indulge in arancini, golden fried rice balls filled with a variety of treats.

Panelle (chickpea fritters) and sfincione (Sicilian pizza) are two examples of the street food available in Palermo. Explore the thriving street markets of Palermo, such as Mercato Ballar, to sample these foods.

PANELLE (CHICKPEA FRITTERS)

SFINCIONE (SICILIAN PIZZA)

Seafood in Catania: **Sardines, wild fennel, and pine nuts** are combined in the pasta dish known as "pasta con le sarde," which is a must-try.

SEAFOOD IN CATANIA

SARDINES

WILD FENNEL

After-Dark Adventures: A Vivacious Nightlife

Sicily's thriving nightlife comes to life as the sun sets. There is something for every taste, from upscale wine bars to busy piazzas.

The ***Vucciria and Ballar markets*** in Palermo become bustling gathering places for locals and tourists to enjoy food, music, and companionship. In a trattoria by the sea, sip some regional wine for a more leisurely evening.

Aperitivo in Taormina

Take part in the Italian custom of aperitivo and savor beverages and small bites while taking in Taormina's breathtaking scenery.

Ortigia Island

Ortigia Island in Syracuse will host live music performances; check the local event listings for details. Local musicians with talent can be found at many venues.

CHAPTER 7

TRANSPORT: Understanding Sicily's Networks

Understanding the island's transportation options is essential to make the most of your trip as navigating Sicily's stunning landscapes and variety of sights is in and of itself an adventure.

Public transportation is effective and readily available.

It is simple to move between towns and regions in Sicily because of its well-connected network of *buses, trains, and ferries.*

Major cities like *Palermo, Catania, and Messina* are connected by trains, which offer beautiful scenery along the journey. Buses are a great way to get to rural and smaller communities that may not be easily accessible by train.

Research schedules and routes in advance, as they can vary based on the season and destination.

Think about getting a Sicily Tourist Card, which grants you access to unlimited public transit and offers savings at attractions.

Taxis and Ride-Sharing: Convenience at Your Fingertips

In urban regions, taxis and ride-sharing services are widely accessible and provide the comfort of door-to-door transportation.

Taxis normally have set rates for popular routes, but it's wise to double-check the fare before setting off on your trip.

If using a ride-sharing app, ensure your app is set up and working before you arrive in Sicily to avoid any connectivity issues.

Car Rentals: Freedom to Explore

Renting a car gives you the flexibility to see Sicily's quaint villages, undiscovered attractions, and stunning scenery at your speed.

Driving gives you the freedom to explore distant locations and go off the beaten path while parking may be scarce in urban hubs.

Make sure you are familiar with the local traffic laws and road signs because they might not be the same as what you are used to.

Especially during the busiest travel seasons, make your automobile rental reservations in advance.

Adventures in Island Hopping with Ferries and Boats

The **Aeolian Islands and the Aegadian Islands**, two nearby islands of Sicily, are reachable by ferry or boat services. These voyages provide an opportunity to take in beautiful sea vistas in addition to providing transportation.

AEGADIAN ISLANDS

AEOLIAN ISLANDS

Check the boat schedules in advance to reserve your spot, especially if you're traveling during the busiest time of year. Be ready for possible weather-related adjustments to ferry schedules.

Walking and Biking: Environmentally Friendly Exploration

Walking or cycling through cities and towns offers a distinctive and environmentally sustainable perspective.

Bike-sharing programs are available in many cities, and walking around will show you local stores, historic landmarks, and undiscovered alleys.

Consider joining a guided walking or cycling tour to gain a better understanding of the history and culture of the area.

CHAPTER 8

RETAIL THERAPY: Sicilian Style Shopping

Start a shopping journey that captures the best of Sicily's rich culture and handiwork.

Markets: Charming Bazaars in Full Swing

Sicily's markets are a colorful tapestry of sights, sounds, and fragrances that completely engulf you in the people and culture of the region.

The vibrant displays of fresh vegetables, spices, and street cuisine at Palermo's Vucciria Market are a sensory overload.

La Pescheria in Catania is a seafood lover's dream come true, where you can see the catch of the day being prepared and taste the real flavors of the sea.

Recommendation

For a wide selection of goods, including regional cheeses, olive oils, apparel, and handcrafted crafts, go to the Ballar Market in Palermo.

Urban treasures in shopping areas

The cities of Sicily are filled with shopping areas where you may browse a range of shops and boutiques.

Corso Umberto, a lovely pedestrian strip in Taormina, is dotted with posh stores that sell everything from clothing to regional handicrafts.

Via Maqueda, a busy boulevard in Palermo, is home to a variety of upscale businesses and creative studios.

Take a stroll through Catania's bustling Via Etnea, which is lined with local stores, foreign retailers, and cafes.

Artisanal Delights is a specialty store.

Shops that highlight Sicilian workmanship should be sought out if you're looking for one-of-a-kind and genuine mementos.

Caltagirone Pottery Studios specializes in intricately crafted ceramics, and Marsala is well-known for its wine cellars and tasting facilities.

For exquisitely crafted bags, belts, and accessories, peruse the artisanal leather goods stores in Sciacca.

Negotiating and Finding Unique Items: The Art of the Deal

In many of the markets and small stores in Sicily, haggling is customary. When purchasing many things or visiting open-air marketplaces, polite haggling might result in great savings.

Prioritize locally produced items like textiles, jewelry, and ceramics while looking for one-of-a-kind finds because they exhibit the island's enduring artistry.

Keep a positive, courteous attitude during haggling. Talk to the vendors; they frequently have intriguing anecdotes to relate about their wares.

Supporting Local Artists Through Ethical Purchases

You can bring a bit of Sicilian culture home by purchasing a local craftsman, and you can also help the community's economy.

The island's history, traditions, and artistic expression are frequently reflected in its handmade items.

For authentic pottery created by expert craftsmen, travel to **Santo Stefano di Camastra**. Your purchase immediately aids in maintaining this age-old custom.

SANTO STEFANO DI CAMASTRA

CHAPTER 9

ITINERARIES AND TOURS: Crafting Your Sicilian Experience

Sicily offers a rich tapestry of experiences waiting to be woven into your journey, whether you have a few days or a few weeks.

Sicilian Highlights (5 Days)

Day 1: Arrive in Palermo, stroll along the coastal promenade in the evening, and discover Palermo's historic core.

PALERMO

COASTAL PROMENADE

Day 2: Explore the magnificent Palermo Cathedral, the equally magnificent Monreale Cathedral, and the Ballar and Vucciria marketplaces.

PALERMO CATHEDRAL

MONREALE CATHEDRA

Day 3: Travel to Agrigento to marvel at the Valley of the Temples, then head to Selinunte to explore ancient ruins.

Day 4: Travel to Taormina, see the Greek Theater, then unwind on the lovely beach at Isola Bella.

Day 5: Take a guided tour to appreciate Mount Etna's unspoiled beauty before leaving Catania.

Sicilian Delights (10 Days)

Follow the highlights itinerary for the first 5 days.

Day 6: Take a tour of the lovely Baroque buildings in the historic town of Ragusa Ibla.

Day 7: Travel to Siracusa to see the Ortigia Island archaeological park and savor the regional seafood.

Day 8: Explore Trapani's old center and the Segesta ancient Greek theater.

Day 9: Spend the day exploring the Aeolian Islands to experience breathtaking scenery and a laid-back island atmosphere.

Day 10: Travel out of Palermo after returning there for some last-minute shopping.

Activities and Tours with a Guide

Historical Walks and Cultural Tours

Join a guided walking tour of Palermo's historic sites, including the Norman Palace and the Capuchin Catacombs.

With the assistance of an experienced guide, tour Siracusa's ancient landmarks and learn about the city's history.

Culinary and Wine Experiences

Go on a culinary tour in Catania, where you may sample regional fare and go to historic marketplaces.

Take part in a Marsala wine-tasting trip to sample the region's well-known wine and see how it is made.

Outdoor Adventures

For panoramic vistas and volcanic landscapes, take a guided trek to the top of

Mount Etna, Europe's highest active volcano.

Take a boat tour of the Aeolian Islands, stopping along the way to bathe in the pristine seas and explore the charming settlements.

Cultural Workshops

Take a cooking class in a traditional Sicilian farmhouse, where you will learn to prepare classic dishes using local ingredients.

Attend a pottery class in *Caltagirone* to learn how to make your ceramic masterpiece under the direction of knowledgeable craftspeople.
In particular, during the busiest traffic times, do your research and reserve guided excursions and activities early.

In addition to offering educational insights, guided tours also give you access to local knowledge and undiscovered treasures that can improve your experience of Sicily.

CHAPTER 10

LOCAL TIPS AND INSIGHTS: Unearthing Sicily's Secrets

Beyond the well-known sites and popular tourist destinations, Sicily is home to a wealth of undiscovered treasures, local knowledge, and cultural depth that are just waiting to be found.

Adopt the "Dolce Far Niente" philosophy: the art of doing nothing.

Sicilians value rest and appreciate the present because of their distinctive outlook on life.

Embrace the idea of *"**dolce far niente**" (**the sweetness of doing nothing**)* while you relax with dinner in a piazza, take in a sunset over the sea, or simply sit in a piazza. Give yourself permission to take it easy and enjoy the beauty all around you.

Locals frequently are privy to their own towns' best-kept secrets. Talk to locals in Sicily to learn about off-the-beaten-path eateries, activities, and beaches that might not be listed in travel guides.

Safety and Deference to Regional Customs

Sicily is generally a safe place to visit, but it's still advisable to pay attention to your surroundings and exercise common sense care.

Respectfully, it is welcomed when people attend churches and other religious buildings by dressed modestly.

Additionally, keep in mind that many businesses and attractions may close in the early afternoon due to the siesta, which is still a part of daily life.

To be respectful and considerate when dealing with locals and touring their areas, be aware of regional traditions and customs.

Immerse yourself in celebrations and festivals.

Sicilian celebrations of culture, tradition, and history take the form of lively festivals. Participating in a local celebration gives you the chance to get closer to the essence of Sicilian identity, whether it's the lively carnival of Acireale or the solemn processions during Holy Week.

Connecting with Locals: Real Interactions

To have a greater grasp of Sicilian culture, interact with the locals. Learn about the lives and stories of store owners, artisans, and restaurant personnel through discussion.

Taking part in a cooking class, art workshop, or expert-led tour can also give you insightful information about the area.

Off-the-Beaten-Path Beauty: Natural Wonders

While the allure of iconic landmarks cannot be denied, Sicily's natural beauty goes well beyond these symbols.

Discover secluded coves, verdant valleys, and peaceful nooks by going off the usual route.

Discover hiking routes in the ***Zingaro*** Nature Reserve that take you to isolated beaches, blue waves, and undeveloped landscapes.

ZINGARO

Environmental Protection: Responsible Travel

Remember to travel responsibly as you take in Sicily's breathtaking scenery. Leave no trace, don't frighten the species, and follow any rules established by regional conservation initiatives.

Consider taking part in beach clean-up activities or lending a hand to regional conservation efforts while you're there.

CHAPTER 11

USEFUL PHRASES: Speaking Sicilian

Engaging with locals in their native language can create memorable interactions and help you connect with the culture on a deeper level.

While Italian is the official language of Sicily, there are some Sicilian phrases and expressions that can enhance your communication and show your appreciation for the local culture.

Here are some basic phrases and their translations:

Hello / Goodbye:
- *Sicilian: "Salutamu" (sah-loo-tah-moo)*
- *Italian: "Ciao" (chow)*

Please / Thank You:

- *Sicilian: "Pi piaciri" (pee pyah-chee-ree)*
- *Italian: "Per favore" (pehr fah-voh-ray) / "Grazie" (grah-tsyeh)*

Yes / No:

- *Sicilian: "Iu" (yoo) / "Nò" (noh)*
- *Italian: "Sì" (see) / "No" (noh)*

Excuse Me / Sorry:

   - *Sicilian: "Scùsami" (skoo-sah-mee)*
   - *Italian: "Mi scusi" (mee skoo-zee) / "Mi dispiace" (mee dee-spee-ah-cheh)*

How are you? / I'm fine:

   - *Sicilian: "Comu stai?" (koh-moo stah-ee) / "Sto beni" (stoh beh-nee)*
   - *Italian: "Come stai?" (koh-meh stai) / "Sto bene" (stoh beh-neh)*

What's your name? / My name is:

   - *Sicilian: "Comu ti chiami?" (koh-moo tee kee-ah-mee) / "Ju mi chiamu" (yoo mee kee-ah-moo)*
   - *Italian: "Come ti chiami?" (koh-meh tee kee-ah-mee) / "Mi chiamo" (mee kee-ah-moh)*

Where is...? / How much does it cost?:

- *Sicilian: "Unni è...?" (oon-nee eh) / "Quanta costa?" (kwahn-tah koh-stah)*
- *Italian: "Dove è...?" (doh-veh eh) / "Quanto costa?" (kwahn-toh koh-stah)*

I don't understand / Can you help me?

- *Sicilian: "Non capisco" (nohn kah-pee-sko) / "Mi puoti jutari?" (mee poo-oh-tee yoo-tah-ree)*
- *Italian: "Non capisco" (nohn kah-pee-sko) / "Mi puoi aiutare?" (mee pwoy ah-yoo-tah-reh)*

While many Sicilians speak Italian, using some Sicilian phrases can be a fun way to engage with locals and show your interest in their culture.

However, keep in mind that Italian is more widely understood, especially in tourist areas.

By incorporating these basic phrases into your conversations, you'll not only enhance your travel experience but also create meaningful connections with the people you meet along your Sicilian journey.

CHAPTER 12

YOUR SICILIAN ODYSSEY MEMORIES: Reflection and Farewell

As your tour of Sicily concludes, pause to consider the impressions, views, and feelings that have characterized your days on this alluring island.

Your journey across Sicily has been weaved together like a tapestry from its past, present, and beautiful scenery. This chapter's conclusion asks you to reflect on your journey, savor the memories, and depart feeling content.

You've toured historic sites that reveal tales of bygone civilizations, enjoyed regional cuisine that reveals tales of tradition, and interacted with kind locals who welcomed you into their community.

Your journey has allowed you to go beyond the obvious and get fully immersed in the rich fabric of Sicilian life.

Travel offers a chance for personal development and transformation beyond simply seeing new places.

Your Sicilian Odyssey has unquestionably extended your viewpoint, deepened your understanding, and left you with a lasting impression.

The memories you bring with you are the real jewels of your travel as you say goodbye to the sunny landscapes and quaint villages. The mosaic that makes up your Sicilian experience includes the jokes told with new acquaintances, the breathtaking views of ancient ruins, and the flavors and scents of Sicilian food.

Sicily has merged with you; it now exists in both your stories and recollections. Your voyage has altered the landscape of your soul, just as the forces of nature have created the landscape of the island.

Remember that Sicily's energy follows you as you exit its shores. Long after your adventure is over, the memories you've made and the lessons you've learned will continue to improve your life. You will always remember the warmth, allure, and beauty of Sicily.

As you bid farewell to Sicily, take a minute to contemplate and write down your thoughts and feelings in a journal. This unique memento will act as a memory of the extraordinary experience you've been on.

You bid Sicily goodbye with a heart full of memories and a spirit affected by its allure knowing that its legacy will live on in your soul forever.

Your Sicilian Odyssey has been more than just a journey across geography; it has also been a journey of the soul, and as you continue your journey, Sicily's spirit follows you, permanently entwined with your own. Sicily, your memories will live on until we cross paths again.